Even in Darkness

For wholesale inquiries contact: paperpeonypress@gmail.com

Printed in China

ISBN - 978-1-952842-43-6

PAPER PEONY PRESS

Even in Darkness

BY: MORGAN CHEEK

Introduction

When I was a little girl, I would get incredibly homesick. It was not the separation from my mom and dad that bothered me most. While I had a close relationship with my parents — and I still do — my homesickness had little to do with my attachment or proximity to them. And, looking back on it, I honestly don't believe my anxiety involved the confines of our house. What was it about being away from home that made my stomach turn and made the world feel suddenly unsafe?

THE DARK.

I have distinct memories of being at summer camp, located a mere fifteen minutes from my neighborhood. During the day, crafts, camp food and walks in nature kept my mind completely at ease. But, around dusk, that time of day where everything began to slow down except the symphony of the crickets, nausea and simultaneous panic would set in. Suddenly, the same people and campground that felt totally comfortable to me during the day began to feel anything but safe as the sun set. I would go through the scenario over and over again as it got closer to lights out. The same physical sensations and mental anguish would take over my brain and body as I wondered if I could survive another night in this terrifying place, which hours before had been quite the haven. And, while we never really talked about it, I could always tell by the quietness that came over us that there were others who were feeling the same way. What was once carefree was now frozen in fear.

Seasons of chronic pain have always given me a remarkably similar feeling.

As someone who typically has a lot to say, grief and suffering have a way of silencing me. In my own deep hurt, I have found the world begins to feel a lot like that campground just after sunset: dark and unfamiliar. In those moments, what once felt warm and secure begins to feel eerily distant. When our souls are full of life's deepest troubles, it can feel as if even our closest friends might actually be our enemies, simply because we are not sure they can understand the level of our pain. And, in the midst of the hardest of hards — even if we've had Sunday School answers prior to it — they go out the window. Desperation has a way of stripping us of all the layers that mask the rawest questions of our hearts.

Suddenly, we are left feeling completely alone. Is this really the place God has for me? Is God even in this? Is God even God? We blush as the contents of our hearts come pouring out. If you have picked up this book, I have a feeling at least some of this resonates with you. And, if you are like me, you have often wondered if these questions are even halfway appropriate to throw out at a Holy God.

I think the Bible argues absolutely yes.

Not only do I believe that Scripture approves, I believe it encourages conversations with God that remove every façade and every perfectly tied-up bow. I believe Scripture invites us to come naked, bruised, confused and completely answerless. We see it in the Psalms, in Job, in Lamentations and in Jeremiah, to name a few. What's even more comforting is that we find this informal, beautiful relationship displayed in Jesus as He cries out to His Father in the Garden of Gethsemane, His sweat and blood asking God for another way through. If this kind of informal conversation is good enough for the Son of God, then surely we have permission to do the same.

Grief is universal.

Within the last two years, I have buried both of my precious daughters. I am sure there is greater pain in this world, but I have yet to find it. During some of our foggiest days — my daughters' diagnoses, hospital stays, or our time with hospice, for example — I found it was really hard to articulate the depths of my heart. I also found, however, that it was necessary to my very survival. And, the intimacy that developed between the Lord and me during those times was the only sanity I had when the bottom dropped out beneath me. I owe this book to those seasons. In these pages, you will find a lot of things; but, one thing you will not find is some kind of formula. There have been many times when I have found myself picking up a book, opening it to a random page and reading just one sentence while asking God to give me a bite of nourishment from those few words. In His grace, sometimes I would find that I actually felt fed from those words. Other times, I would slam the book shut, discouraged and feeling abandoned because, in spite of what I longed for, nothing seemed to sink into my weary soul. We intentionally did not label this book with specific days or much structure for that very reason. When your entire being is already feeling heavy, the last thing you need is someone to tell you one more way to do one more thing. There is no right way to read these pages. I trust the Holy Spirit to work in whatever method He chooses. And, even when I become suspicious of that, His fulfillment is still the same. His track record in my life has been perfect. That's not to say it has always felt that way. But, I know it is perfect because He is God, and I am not. And, that's a good thing. He has sustained me through the unimaginable, time and time again, even on the days I have doubted that He would. I am learning to believe this is because God is holding me, not the other way around.

SO BACK TO THE DARKNESS.

My hope and prayer for this book is that it will be like a wall in a dark room. Let me explain. You know that feeling when you wake up in the middle of the night in an unfamiliar room and need to get out of bed? When you are at home, it isn't a big deal. Your frame of reference will get you to the bathroom or sink without much thought. But, if you are in a place you have never been before, you are left to reach for something that offers some sort of stability to get you where you need to go. I want the offerings in this book to be like a wall in the dark, guiding you to move forward. I pray you will be able to take a breath — if not a deep one, a breath, still — as God uses these gut-wrenching, real words to help usher you forward for one more second. And, during the moments when you cannot seem to find a wall and you are vulnerable, standing alone in this dark and strikingly foreign place, I pray you hear His voice inviting you to simply sit down in the night and weep. I have often said that during times of intense grief, it has been hard for me to form complete sentences. I am thankful God does not ask me to. He actually tells me it's okay for my words to be few. He doesn't throw out a million words at me either. He often speaks to me in simple phrases, letting His living and active words penetrate my heart so that I am able to press on. I have included several Scriptures, some phrases in bold, that have been soul-bolstering to me in some of my darkest days. Consider them little sips of water in a dry desert. Some of the words ahead will be heavy and certainly not eloquent, and that is okay. The darkness is as light with Him. God meets us wherever we are. We must be comfortable with the Comforter in order to be comforted by Him. And, how do you get comfortable with someone? You show up as is, time and time again. There will be several prompts in the pages ahead. I say, "If you want" and "If not" because I want to take the pressure off of what will inevitably come. If it doesn't resonate with you, don't do it. Simple as that.

Before we move on, can I just say I am sorry for your pain? For whatever reason someone deemed this book appropriate for you, I am just so sorry. Along with that, I am looking forward, on your behalf, for the depth of relationship that can come from allowing God to meet you in the dark. I won't give you some salt-in-a-wound platitude, telling you better days are coming. Truthfully? I have not always found that to be true; and, I have usually found it to be annoyingly unhelpful, regardless. But, I do believe that somehow He is producing something in each of our lives that will make this all feel light and momentary in the now and then. My prayer for you in the here and now? Rest in the embrace of the hands whose love bled for you. He is carrying you with those same scarred hands, whether circumstances or emotions speak of it or not. I know it is true. Not because I have always believed it on any given day, but because I have lived it and experienced it in the middle of my own life — *even in darkness.*

Your eyes saw my unformed substance; in Your book were written, every one of them, the days that were formed for me, when as yet there was none of them. —Psalm 139:16

"Your eyes saw my unformed substance; in Your book were written, every one of them, the days that were formed for me, when as yet there was none of them"

Psalm 139:16

I have come to these words before. When I was younger, I read them like a neatly played-out poem. Oh, good, I would think. God knows everything. But, now the words just seem confusing.

God, You tell us that You know everything; but, even this?! I thought these truths were supposed to comfort me. Instead, I'm just perplexed by the reality that You have seen all my struggles and yet somehow, You have chosen to announce them good.

We sing it confidently at church. We say it to each other, the words coming off our tongues like syrup: God is good. But, these words do not taste sweet to me right now, God — far from it. Today feels tasteless at best and poisonous at most. And honestly, God, I feel suspicious of You. How can You look down at me, knowing all that You know, and say that these struggles are worth applauding? There is just too much rubble here. How could this pain be producing anything except for more pain?

But, then I remember that Your ways are not mine. I am confident that You are looking through the lenses of eternity, not just a snapshot of time. So, when I think about the concept of You saying that all of this is good, I want to remember You are not seeing these struggles the same way that I am seeing them. You hate suffering. You died to overcome it. You are not some malicious god giving a standing ovation to evil. No, that's the Enemy of my soul. That's not You. If You wrote all of my days before they began, and since the Bible says that You are perfect in all of Your ways, then I can rest knowing that eventually I will see this day as a part of the beautiful masterpiece that You created it to be. I do not have to like my current circumstances to know this is true. Lord, help me to have hope for what You say is eventually coming. Help me to know that the weight of this day does not have to smother me in light of Your future promises for me. I do not have to rest in this horrible suffering; but, may I rest in You in the midst. Thank You for not leaving me. Thank You for never letting me go and for telling me that every day is a part of Your perfect plan, even when everything in clear view feels like chaos. Help me to trust You more, here in this place. Only You can do that, God. I have nothing to offer but myself.

IF YOU WANT...
Read Psalm 139 in its entirety, asking God to reveal parts of His character to you that are currently hard for you see.

IF NOT...
During the moments when it is hard to breathe today, whisper this truth to yourself:
"Every one of them — even today — has been written by the God who is love."

Give me not up to the will of my adversaries

—Psalm 27:12a—

"Give me not up to the will of my adversaries"

Psalm 27:12a

What a place to be, Lord.

I sit here attempting to believe that You are for me, wanting to know that You are in control and that You are the Sovereign Ruler above all things. Yet, I doubt it at times. I doubt because I am human, and what I see seems to be so entirely different from what You say is true. How long, O Lord? How much longer will this pain and these circumstances seem like they are eating me up? It feels like my soul is being consumed from the inside out because of these challenges that keep appearing over and over again. If I felt Your peace that passes understanding, I think I would trust that everything will be okay. But, my faith is weak as I try to live in these moments. It seems as if Your promises of filling me up are failing. I do not feel filled, Lord. I feel empty, dry and consumed by it all. Lord, be near. I need You. I have so many fears about Your absence. But maybe that is the grace. Maybe this feeling — that in spite of everything in front of me, I know deep down You are for me — is, in fact, the miracle. You will sustain me, in spite of myself, despite what my emotions are screaming at me and what the world might say. "Where is Your God?" I hear it being whispered to my weary soul. Lord, I am afraid of believing these lies. Help me to trust You in the midst of it all. Help me to know You are in this place, even here. Help my unbelief. *Give me not up, God.* Without You, I am nothing.

IF YOU WANT...

1). Look through Psalm 27. Make a list of what you think God wants to do in our lives versus what the Enemy aims to do in our lives. (Hint: Look for verbs.)

2). Read Psalm 27 aloud, replacing "I," "me" and "my" with your name.

IF NOT...

Write the following short prayer on a sticky note, your hand or a mirror so that you will see it frequently.

I am Yours, forever, God.

a lamp shining in a dark place

2 Peter 1:19

"And we have the prophetic word more fully confirmed, to which you will do well to pay attention as to a lamp shining in a dark place, until the day dawns and the morning star rises in your hearts"

2 Peter 1:19

Lord, today feels dark.

I'm trying my best to find You in this season. The darkness seems brighter than Your light right now. Why is that? This morning, I lit every candle within sight. I needed the reminder that the light is here, that You are here. There is a flame in me that I know will not be quenched because You say it is so. Lord, You are. That's it. That is all that really matters. My soul knows this in spite of the darkness that seems to cover me. You promised that dark and light are the same to You. So, perhaps when I see the blackness of the darkest night or the brightness of the brightest day, it is not relevant. It feels important to let You know what You already know: that I am hurting in the darkness. My pain feels incurable and deep. I do not see a way out of this. I do not understand why every season of life lately has to be so full of trial. Even the world around me feels so broken, so Godless. Yet, I know You are here. As I watch this flame flicker in front of me, I am reminded that You are not going anywhere; and that even in these dark hours You are producing something whose glory will blind me in the heavenly realms because of its beauty. You create beauty from ashes. That is what You do. That is who You are.

Yet, here I am today, in pain.

God, would You lead me to see the light? Would You usher me into the reality that is You? I know You are more real than the breath that I breathe. You are my very life! And, You tell me that it is in remembering the Gospel — the reality of Christ — that the light that is shining can be seen by my heart. Help me to fix my eyes on this right now.

IF YOU WANT...
Find the darkest room in your house, turn off all the lights, and either light a candle or turn on a flashlight. Quiet your mind and heart, and simply look at the light for as much time as you have available. Ask God to speak truth to your soul in these moments.

IF NOT...
Repeat this to yourself as many times as you need today:

God's lamp is always shining.

he has made me desolate; he bent his bow and set me as a target for his arrow

Lamentations 3:10-12

"He is a bear lying in wait for me, a lion in hiding; he turned aside my steps and tore me to pieces; he has made me desolate; he bent his bow and set me as a target for his arrow"

Lamentations 3:10–12

It feels like I am reading the Bible for the first time. I never knew about these verses that talk about Your sovereignty in all things suffering. I am not sure why I never considered this. After all, You sent Your Son to suffer and die. When He asked for another way — Your answer was through. If the perfect Son of God can say, "nevertheless," and trust in those moments, then surely I can as well. But, Lord, You know. You know the excruciating pain that I am feeling each moment. Yet, You lead me to these words as I sit in the depths of my pain. Lamentations 3 makes it abundantly clear. "He has" is said over and over, but the words following it sound like wounds from an enemy rather than comfort from a friend. How in the world can I trust You when I know You intend to allow so much pain and suffering? Sometimes it feels crazy to have faith in a God who inflicts His Beloved over and over again. Yet in the verses that follow, You also make this clear: You do not afflict from the heart. And, the suffering You allow is considered light and momentary when compared to what You are doing with it. You created me when I was not. You died for me when death would have been the final story for me. You must — You must — YOU MUST love me because nothing else makes sense. And, there is something about accepting the fact that You have permitted these gut-wrenching, awful things that spurs my heart to remember that You are doing something with all that You allow. Not one thing You are doing will be wasted, even when it feels like nothing but rubble. God, help me to accept that the One who loves me also could have chosen to stop this horrific pain, yet didn't. Help me to know that You would never place something in my life if beautiful things were not coming from it. I do not have to see it to know it is true. May I sit in this discomfort and know You sit right here with me. Help me to remember some of the most beautiful "He has" statements in Your Word:

He has promised never to leave or to forsake.
He has died for me when I was helpless.
He has forgiven all my sins.
He has promised to satisfy me with Himself for all eternity.
He has given me Himself, His very life, forever.

Thank You for this joy You are spurring in my heart, God. Only You are able.

IF YOU WANT...
Read through Lamentations 3. While thinking of some of your own pain and suffering, replace some of the words in Lamentations 3 with words from your own journey. Feel free to be as explicit as the words in the chapter. Do not be afraid to tell it like it is; He already knows. Speak it aloud or write it. Once you have done so, make verses 19-33 a personal prayer.

IF NOT...
Read Lamentations 3:31-33 aloud. I am asking God right now, on your behalf, to give you a glimpse of the truth of those words today.

For God alone, O my soul, wait in silence, for my hope is from Him. He only is my rock and my salvation, my fortress; I shall not be shaken

Psalm 62:5-6

"For God alone, O my soul, wait in silence, for my hope is from Him. He only is my rock and my salvation, my fortress; I shall not be shaken"

Psalm 62:5-6

I'm not very good at being silent. It is even harder to be quiet when I feel like an injustice is happening to myself or someone I love. Father, this all just feels so wrong. It feels wrong that I am in a place of such pain. You say that You are a God of justice, but where is the justice here?? I am confused and don't know what to do next. I want to trust You. I long to be someone who laughs at the days to come because I know that, ultimately, the battle has already been won. Lord, help me to get there. It scares me to think about the cost that might come in order to accomplish a deeper trust in me. It always feels like the second I pray for more of something from You, a loss is evident. I long to trust You with the losses, no matter how great they may seem. Help me to know that You are producing things greater than I could imagine with all the empty places. I want to know, beyond a shadow of a doubt, that You are filling my heart with Yourself. Lord, teach me to trust that wherever I see ruins, You see a masterpiece being produced. Broken is not broken in Your hands. Not only that, You say You are near to the brokenhearted. So even when I don't sense Your presence, may I trust that You are all the more near. Everyone and everything else is coming up dry in this place. Nothing is making me feel better — not even my go-to habits or band-aids or coping mechanisms. But, You alone have hope for me in these ashes. I want to know that You are putting Yourself between me and the chasm in front of me — not only surrounding me, but standing in the gap. That is who You are. Even in the dark, I know this to be true. Thank You for revealing Yourself to me, God. Teach me to trust You more. And, when I look back on this season, whether on earth or in heaven, may I look back and confidently say that *He only* got me through the dark. Thank You for never leaving my side.

IF YOU WANT...
Take a look at Psalm 62 and write down all the words used to describe God. Look up the definition of those words. If you'd like, use the contents in the back of a bible (or the internet!) and find other verses that have those same descriptive words for God.

IF NOT...
Repeat this phrase throughout the day: *He only* can get me through this.

The secret things belong to the Lord our God, but the things that are revealed belong to us...
Deuteronomy 29:29

"The secret things belong to the Lord our God, but the things that are revealed belong to us and to our children forever, that we may do all the words of this law"

Deuteronomy 29:29

I hate not knowing.
I hate not understanding the "why" behind the "what."

It has always been this way for me.
Lord, I feel like if I understood what You were doing, then I could accept it.
What You are doing right now, Lord, is impossible for me to understand.

There is nothing about my current situation that makes any kind of sense to me. And, honestly, I wonder if I would even be able to comprehend the future if You explained it to me. If it is greater than I could ask for or imagine, then it must be bigger than I can grasp. At times, it feels like this will eventually drive me crazy. But, You say You have me in the palm of Your hand — that You are holding me fast. So, instead of trying to figure it all out, I want to rest in You and what I know is true. I have felt You sustain me in the most unimaginable circumstances. I have watched You lift people from rock-bottom and carry them up from the depths of their own hell. I have known You to be a friend when I found no other. And, Your word tells me that You love me unconditionally and eternally. They tell me — You tell me — that You will never let me go. So, when I cannot understand what You are doing with my mind, may I trust You with my heart. Deep down, I know that You are good. I know that You are kind. I know that You won't leave me in this dark place forever. Does it already feel like forever? Yes, it absolutely does. But, I will see Your goodness — whether on this side of eternity or the next. And, You will wipe away all of these tears. Thank You, God, for revealing this to me. Thank You for being so patient with me as I flounder through trust. While there seems to be an infinite number of *secret things*, thank You for helping me choose to believe that these *secret things* are too good to be true; but, yet are true.

Thank You for loving me, my God.
Thank You for Your patience with me.
Thank You for grace that knows no bounds.

Thank You for promising that in eternity, these mysterious happenings, which currently make me want to shake my fist in Your direction, will be the very things that bring me to my knees with redeemed hands raised in praise.

IF YOU WANT...
Read 1 Corinthians 13:12. Talk with God about the things you cannot wait to see and fully understand.

IF NOT...
Picture what you think heaven — a secret place with secret things — will be like and look like. Don't hold back and don't overthink it. Let yourself dream and imagine. You may want to even draw a picture or write out some of the details.

Jesus Wept
John 11:35

"Jesus Wept"

John 11:35

I feel so numb. It feels as if I either have no more tears to cry or that the tears are afraid to come because once they do, they are not going to stop. Has that ever happened? Has someone ever died from crying for so long, so hard, that they just could not stop? Right now, I just want this all to go away. I am so sick of the unknown. I am tired of trusting. I am longing to be free from the pain that is my life. How am I supposed to believe You care when I am in the same place day after day? The wound feels absolutely incurable. If I thought there was a place to go to relieve the pain, believe me, I would go. But, there is nothing. No one, nowhere is offering any sort of relief. Lord, where else can I go? You are my only comfort. Would You comfort me here? Sometimes it feels like we are playing some game of cat and mouse. I blush as I write it. But, You know. It seems like You want to stay close enough to make me want You, yet far enough for me to have to be frustrated as I seek You. Why is that? Why does it seem that in the places that hurt the deepest, You cause me to know You are here, but do not allow me to feel the balm of Your presence? When You finally chose to show up for Mary and Martha, Lazarus was already dead. You knew what You were about to do. You knew that no time is too late when You are involved. But, You still cried. You did not cry robotically or controlled either. You wept. I imagine the emotion welling up inside You, pouring out with sobs and screams, Your face stained with salty tears, verklempt with compassion. Both Martha and Mary felt the things I feel today. Lord, why didn't You show up? Why are You not showing up when I need You most? The whisper behind it all is this: Are You really who I hope You to be? Father, that's my authentic question today. I wish my faith was stronger and greater than that, but here we are. Yet, in the midst of all the suspicions, You still raised Lazarus from the dead. Did he die again eventually? Of course he did. But, You made Yourself known in those moments; and, really, that is what I need today, too. I just need to know You are here in these moments. Lord, give me a glimpse of that. Give me a mustard seed of faith in who You are. May I know You are not a distant God, but that You weep with me here in this valley. Come quickly, Lord. I am hanging on by a thread.

IF YOU WANT…

Read John 11. Pay attention to all of the different people in the chapter. In this current season of your life, who do you relate to most and why? What would change if you trusted that Jesus was reliable in this chapter in the story of your life?

IF NOT…

Picture Jesus weeping beside you. Know that whether you believe it or not in any given moment, He is.

Whom have I in heaven but you? And nothing on earth I desire besides you

Psalm 73:35

"Whom have I in heaven but You? And there is nothing on earth I desire besides you"

Psalm 73:35

I keep reading these words over and over, waiting for them to feel better. I wish I could simply veer past them like an item in a buffet line that doesn't look appetizing. But, I can't. I can't because they are words in Your Holy Book that bother me. And, when I find something You have allowed to be divinely written that doesn't sit right, I know that means I need to accept it. It seems like David wrote these words so flippantly. It's like he casually threw this out there without any question: God, You are all I need on earth or in heaven. And, at one point, I would have naively spouted out those same words. Yet, now, to tell You that all I want is in heaven would be a lie because there are large pieces of my heart that supposedly reside there. It seems odd that You would want us to only care about You. Nothing I read about You sounds like a leader only out for Himself. What I read is quite the opposite. Yet, why would You want us to not long for the very creation You made? How do we make You the center of our universe without ignoring or despising the gifts You have given us?

I need some context. I don't need something that will change the words. I need something that will give me an idea of how another human being (one who lost a child, might I add!) could so confidently say these things that are so challenging for my own heart. I have read the verses before, and they feel like both new lenses and medicinal ointment for my soul. David himself began this Psalm very confused. He wrote it because he was frustrated with what seemed contradictory to him. He was feeling as if people who didn't care about God lived easy lives, while those like himself — who were desperately trying to give God their all — seemed to suffer even more. This sounds so very familiar to me. God, You know.

And, yet, David goes on to express a version of these words in verses 16-17: "It was painful and heart-weary for me to understand why all this was so — until I went into the sanctuary of God."

I think there are some things I will never understand until I meet You face-to-face. Yet, because of Christ, You have given me full access to Your throne room where somehow I already sit. And, faith is just that: believing in the unseen. Who hopes for what he already sees? I don't know why faith is the thing that You ask for; but the reality is, like David, I can choose to have faith. The more I know You, the more I am going to realize that nothing compares. Whom have I in heaven *but You*?

Today, that is enough. Let that be enough, God.

IF YOU WANT...
Read through Psalm 73 and talk with God about the things that resonate within your own heart.

IF NOT...
Pray to trust in Psalm 73:26: My flesh and my heart may fail, but God is the strength of my heart and my portion forever. Even when our very self fails us, He does not.

For now we see in a mirror dimly, but then face to face. Now I know in part; then I shall know fully, even as I have been fully known.

1 Corinthians 13:12

"For now we see in a mirror dimly, but then face to face. Now I know in part; then I shall know fully, even as I have been fully known"

1 Corinthians 13:12

Now versus *then*. Sometimes, Lord, it seems like such a sharp contrast. Before the beginning of time, You saw it all and claimed it to be good. Then, the fall happened, and everything becomes confusing to me. If You are sovereign, why all of that? Everywhere in Your Word seems clear to me: You are in control of every millisecond of time since before the beginning of time. If this is true, and if You also hate evil, how does this all work together? I don't know, and I'm almost certain that I'm not going to know on this side of heaven. Right *now*, there are parts of Your word that just do not make sense to me. But, that is the thing. You have also made it crystal clear that Your ways are higher than mine and that, truly, I was not meant to comprehend it all. I wish I could just take that in as truth and let it stick. But, it is so hard to trust when the broken abounds. 1 Corinthians 13 is a chapter often read at weddings. It's all about love. God, Your Word says that You are love. You are patient, enduring and all the things in between. If this is true, then it seems You can be trusted with the *now* because You promise us nothing less than Yourself in the *then*. Lord, I do not know what to do, but my eyes are, in fact, on You. I long to fully understand the story You have written for me. I want to see how this all turns out. Sometimes, I feel like if You would give me a greater glimpse of that, I would be able to persevere through this part a little more. Yet, You promise that You are providing all that I need to be sustained in this moment. You are a good, good Father in spite of some of the things I see. I know this is true. My feelings are not the full story. This chapter is not the full story. You are getting the glory and one day, I will see it in completion because You are seeing it to completion.

Help me to trust You, in this place, *now*.

IF YOU WANT...
Turn to Hebrews 11 and read through the reality of faith. Notice that the temporal outcome of faith looked very different for each person mentioned; yet, the eternal outcome of faith was the same. How can you apply this to your life *now*?

IF NOT...
Repeat these words to yourself today: *Now* is not the full story.

If in Christ we have hope in this life only, we are of all people most to be pitied. But in fact Christ has been raised from the dead, the firstfruits of those who have fallen asleep

1 Corinthians 15:19-20

"If in Christ we have hope in this life only, we are of all people most to be pitied. But in fact Christ has been raised from the dead, the firstfruits of those who have fallen asleep"

1 Corinthians 15:19-20

Oh, the internet. I find myself encouraged yet frustrated by the so-called people of God. The problem is not my phone's fault. It is not some company's issue. It is our own hearts. The fact that You created us with knowledge of all things blows my mind, God. We are such fickle children. And, God, I confess that some of Your children — my supposed brothers and sisters — drive me crazy. I question their legitimacy as if it is mine to question. I am just so tired of watching people preach "the good life" found in Jesus. That is not what I find in Your Bible! From my view, Your Word seems to teach sharing in sufferings much more than seven steps to happiness. The people of God in biblical times seemed to embrace suffering. But, now I feel like Your name is treated like that of a genie or plastic surgeon — there to give us what we want, when we want it. I think this bothers me for both good and bad reasons. The truth is that I want You represented as Yourself. I want people to know You as the God who allows trials to come to enhance our dependence on You. I long for others to understand what it looks like to know that sometimes, Your will be done is not earthly healing, but a heavenly reward. The trouble with that is suddenly we can begin to think that our works are the story; but, that is not right either! I am frustrated. I feel like I cannot even explain it correctly to You. Maybe that is the point. Constant reminders tell me that only Jesus can save us from ourselves. Like Paul, I find great comfort in these words: If in Christ we have hope *in this life only*, we are of all people most to be pitied. That is not "bless your heart" language. No. That is a downright bold proclamation that reminds me that sharing in Your sufferings only makes sense if what I believe about You is actually true. If not, the world should feel very sorry for me. Yet, the next sentence spurs me on because he continues saying, "But in fact, Christ has been raised from the dead." This means that we should not be pitied because You are somehow causing these horrible things to work together for good. I do not have to understand it to know it is true. Father, I pray to be kept in Your perfect will today. I want to remember that this life is only a breath, and that You are doing something here and now. I love You, Lord. Be near. Also, I am sorry that I do not always love Your children as I should, or when I spend more time judging than extending the very grace that I need. You are always more. Thanks be to God.

IF YOU WANT...
Read 1 Corinthians 15. If Christ's death and resurrection was not true, why should Christians be most pitied? If it is true, why should they not?

IF NOT...
Pray this simple prayer: God, help me to believe that Christ's resurrection is true.

Praise the Lord! for it is good to sing praises to our God; for it is pleasant, and a song of praise is fitting —Psalm 147:1

"Praise the Lord! For it is good to sing praises to our God; for it is pleasant, and a song of praise is fitting"

Psalm 147:1

Fitting. The word fitting means appropriate. You are the God of all the universe. If You were not, there would be nothing. You created the sun, the moon, the stars, the birds of the air and the fish of the sea. You made plants both for beauty and sustenance, and everything in between. You spoke and it all came to be. You also determined that people would be made in Your very image. If You had not breathed life into us, we would not be. So, it does seem suitable that we would praise You for this. Except some days, the pain I feel is so deep that the fact that You created me feels more like a curse than a blessing. There are days that I feel as if I would rather be dead. The ache that I feel because of the struggles You claim to have allowed is an ache I have never known. Why don't You always feel near to me in my brokenness? It seems like these moments are the ones You would choose to draw closer to me; yet, You feel so distant. I do not want to think You are cruel. I know You are not. Deep down, my soul knows that well. You have been so good to me. You have never left me, even when it feels like You might have. I know this is true despite the emotions that sometimes tell me otherwise. Is it the Enemy telling me these things or my very own flesh? Who knows? All I know is that when I become so consumed with what is in front of me, I can easily forget Your faithfulness in the past and Your promises for the future. Lord, help me to see You and find You more clearly right here in this place. Help me to stop trying to understand what You are doing and, instead, simply rest in who You are. I need You. I need You for more than just answers and changes in circumstance — although that would be extremely great right now. I can sense You drawing me closer to You even in the silence — maybe even most especially in the silence. I know You are intentional in all You do and that You would never leave me. Help me to trust this more today. Help me to trust You more today. When I picture praise, I picture smiling and lightheartedness. This can feel like nails on a chalkboard in times like these. Yet, coming to You with open hands and a heart that longs to know You more is praise in itself. *Praise is fitting*. Maybe this is the praise that You speak of. May I praise You with all that I am and all that I have. My weakness is Your strength. I have seen and known this. May it be so, even here.

IF YOU WANT...

What comes to mind when you hear the word praise? Is it positive or negative? Is it formal or informal? What would it look like to authentically praise God in the sad and dark places of life?

IF NOT...

Write these words down somewhere: I do not have to feel happy to praise You, God.

We do not know what to do, but our eyes are on you.

2 Chronciles 20:12

"O our God, will You not execute judgment on them? For we are powerless against this great horde that is coming against us. We do not know what to do, but our eyes are on You"

2 Chronicles 20:12

It was their worship that defeated the enemy. King Jehoshaphat and the people of Judah and Jerusalem did not seem particularly excited or even brave, considering the great horde that was going to come against them. Suddenly, some guy named Jahaziel (why am I just seeing him?) told the people that God told Jahaziel that He was going to fight for them, and that all they had to do was trust Him. And, that was it. They just did. Sometimes, I sense a struggle in the stories of the Bible. This one just seems as simple as that. Why am I not experiencing this in my current darkness? It feels like if You would just send me a Jahaziel, I would take a sigh of relief and be able to move forward. Yet, instead, I feel alone and frozen in the next steps. How long, O Lord? As I read these words again, something new sticks out. The first step the people took was to come to You and admit they had no idea what to do. I am definitely there. I know I am powerless against what is in front of me. Yet, the only other thing they did was fix their eyes on You. That's it. What would it look like for me to fix my eyes on You right now? So often, I want to fast forward to see the results of my darkness. I want the face-to-face when You have called me to the faith-to-faith. You were not standing in front of the people of Judah and Jerusalem. You did not send an angel down to speak in this particular situation. So, the eyes the people had on You must have been simply the eyes of their hearts. As I am standing in front of what feels like decisions that are both extremely heavy and out of my control, yet necessary for me to make, would You set the eyes of my heart on You? Instead of looking at what I can see, teach me to see the unseen.

I do not know what to do Lord, but I am choosing to put my eyes on You.

Would You meet me in this place today?

IF YOU WANT...
Spend some time praying Ephesians 1:15-23 over yourself, asking God to open the eyes of your heart to the things unseen.

IF NOT...
Admit to God that you do not know what to do.

Be strong and courageous. Do not be frightened and do not be dismayed, for the Lord your God is with you wherever you go —Joshua 1:9

"Be strong and courageous. Do not be frightened, and do not be dismayed, for the Lord your God is with you wherever you go"

Joshua 1:9

I feel like, so often, people focus on the do-not-be-afraid part of this verse. But, dismayed? That is what stands out to me this morning. I woke up, feeling butterflies in my stomach and jittery before my coffee. The details ahead do not necessarily scare me; yet, I do feel unnerved. Opposed. Confused. When I think of fear, I think of monsters under my bed or driving in a bad thunderstorm — the same feeling I used to get before a tug-of-war game at a school field day. As silly as that sounds, there are not many things that bring out an "I'm scared" emotion. But, dismay? How could I not be discouraged in this place? When I look at the circumstances in front of me, all I can see is disappointment after disappointment. It feels as if I am trusting You to come through and then the next thing I know, the second I take a breath, the bottom falls out again. Why does this life have to be so hard? I understand the importance of a few trials. But, this? All I am asking for is a small season of time where I can rest. Is that too much to ask from the One who supposedly loves me, God?

My mind goes to the cross and quickly back to the Garden of Gethsemane. If You were sweating blood, it seems as if You just might have been a little discouraged? How is this any different? Yet, nevertheless, those were Your words. I am confident You would not ask us to do something You were not capable of doing. That does not make any sense. So, it seems that while You were in great agony, maybe that pain was simply pain and not distrust. In fact, it had to have been so. I am grateful to see You in the Garden. I am thankful to be able to visualize You longing for a different way, but accepting with open hands the lot in front of You. For joy. You endured for the joy of saving me, saving us. And, the very God that says, "do not be dismayed" is the One who bled and died, and now sits resurrected on the throne. Therefore, when discouragement creeps into my heart, I must fight it. Not because this is not hard. This is hard; really, really hard. And, You know that because You know more about it than any other being ever will or ever could. But, You tell me to not be unnerved because You know the full story. You have seen it to completion, and You are here with me, fighting on my behalf. Therefore, I can confidently step forward, no matter what the day holds. I do not have to like what is in front of me to accept it as Your best. And, my feelings do not dictate what I know is the truth. Lord, help me to bring my discouragement to You. Give me the Daily Bread to hope in what is to come. Help me to know that no matter what, the victory is Yours. It was the cross that made the change. Thanks be to God.

IF YOU WANT...
Find some synonyms for the word "dismay" and look up those words, either in the back of your bible or on the internet. Meditate on some other verses that talk about why we should not be dismayed.

IF NOT...
Pray this simple prayer: God, telling me to not be dismayed is not invalidating my current circumstances; but, rather further validating Your victory in all things. Thank You for this. May it be so.

May God be gracious to us and bless us and make His face to shine upon us

— Psalm 67:1 —

"May God be gracious to us and bless us and make His face to shine upon us"

Psalm 67:1

Lord, I confess this word has driven me crazy in recent years. This idea of You blessing us was great to me when I was in years of feeling fortunate and blessed. I can remember praying these words, "God, be with those less fortunate than us." What did I mean by that? Was I praying for people with less money? Less stuff? Less happiness? I am not sure. I also recall praying this a lot, "Thank You for blessing us so much." I heard it from the masses: Count your blessings. And, I would start with all the typical things: breath in my lungs, food, shelter. I would go on to think through all the "little things," as they say. These days, I am not sure I even know what a blessing is anymore. I still have all the things listed above. Yet, they do not feel as much like gifts anymore because I have realized they just do not fill my cup. Beyond that, affliction after affliction has been pouring over me like water. Waves upon waves of loss, and hard. Is this what it means to be blessed?

As I continue to read the Psalm, I remember the Beatitudes. When I think about what You call blessed, I am reminded that it is quite different from the world's version. Spiritual blessings — the eternal ones — they are the ones that last. And, if these horrible things are producing more spiritual blessings — if I could see the finished products of these trials — would I see it all as one big blessing from You? Somehow, my heart says yes. I want to believe this, Lord. I want to trust that Your seemingly upside-down Kingdom is actually right side up in the scheme of eternity. All Your works are good. All Your ways are good. I do not have to see it to believe it. I do not want to be calloused to the word "blessed." I want to look to Your Word to know what it really means to be fortunate. Lord, help me to see it Your way. Help me to know the secret treasures of this dark place and to be spurred to praise, somehow, someway. Only You can accomplish this in me. Only You can help me to say, "*Bless us*, Lord," and trust You know what that looks like. I will wait for You.

IF YOU WANT...
Turn to Matthew 5:1-12. Read through what Jesus pronounced as blessed. Which statement do you relate to most in this season and why?

IF NOT...
A simple prayer: Lord, thank You that Your version of blessed does not line up with the world's. Help me to trust that You are who You say You are. Amen.

The Lord is slow to anger and great in power, and the Lord will by no means clear the guilty. His way is in whirlwind and storm, and the clouds are the dust of His feet. –Nahum 1:3

"The Lord is slow to anger and great in power, and the Lord will by no means clear the guilty. His way is in whirlwind and storm, and the clouds are the dust of His feet"

Nahum 1:3

I looked up its definition but didn't have to. This idea of a whirlwind makes complete sense to me because I feel like my life has been spinning out of control for years, despite my own futile efforts to make it stop. Lord, why is Your way in the whirlwind and storm? Those two words describe confusion and chaos to me. I feel like You saying that you prefer the dynamics of turbulent times does not line up with who I think you are. Why would you want hard things for Your people? If we are Your beloved children, how is this not a stone? How can this possibly be good for us? I see no good in this. None. I think about a storm — the darkness and pounding of rain and hail, the strikes of lightning and roars of thunder. As humans, we have absolutely no ability to stop these things. Yet, they stop. At some point, the sun comes back out and the ground is full of water. I once read that thunderstorms are crucial because they balance the energy of the atmosphere. They also provide a large portion of our water supply. The truth is that my way is not the way of the *whirlwind and storm*. If it were up to me, I would only have predictable skies and sunny journeys. Yet, I know that it has been amid the hypothetical tsunamis of my life, and the life of those around me, that things have been able to grow. My dependence on You would be in a much shallower place had You not taken me to deep waters. Maybe Your way is there because You know that is where You meet us most intimately. Your love is so much greater than I could ever fathom. You are comfortable using difficult things to produce the greater things. You do not expect me to understand it now. How could I? I am a mere human who has more questions than answers on any given day. Yet You are God alone. May I not get so focused on the *whirlwind and the storm* that I lose sight of the One controlling it all. Lord, help me to trust You. Help me to know that because no paths are uncharted by You, I can rest easy even when I do not know the way. May I fix my eyes on eternity and the reality that Your promise is coming. May I know You are doing something even when my eyes cannot see. May it be well with my soul during what feels like a nightmare. Lord, You are good. Your mercy endures forever. Please be near.

IF YOU WANT...

What type of weather feels most chaotic and powerful to you? Picture yourself in the middle of that storm. Imagine what it would feel like to be present in an F5 tornado or a category 5 hurricane (or think back on a time this has happened if you have gone through it before). Engage all your senses. Then, envision the Lord in front of, behind and with you during that moment. Picture His calm, confident sovereignty in the chaos. Ask God to speak to you about your current circumstances.

IF NOT...

Say this aloud or in your heart: God, help me to see You in the whirlwind and storm.

The Lord will fulfill His purpose for me; your steadfast love, O Lord, endures forever. Do not forsake the work of your hands

Psalm 138:8

"The Lord will fulfill His purpose for me; Your steadfast love, O Lord, endures forever. Do not forsake the work of Your hands"

Psalm 138:8

Lord, You said it on the cross. Why, O, why have You forsaken me? I do not think I will ever understand the complexities of the Trinity on this side of heaven. When you said Father, Son, Holy Spirit — three in one — You were speaking to Yourself. There are parts of my heart that understand it and parts that just do not. And, I guess that is okay. I recognize that a God that is worthy of worship is not going to be One whose ways are always comprehensible to a human being. Yet, if the God of the universe was able to cry out these words, I guess it is acceptable that I do. I am not even sure what I mean by that. You know my heart. You know me better than I know myself, and you are familiar with all my thoughts and all my ways. I might as well admit them and own them. Is the reality of feeling forsaken an admittance or error? Or, is it just a part of being human? I am not sure; and, I am becoming more comfortable with not understanding it all and with simply clinging to what I do partially grasp. So, back to the whole forsaken thing. I do not really feel completely abandoned by You. Honestly, I just feel sad. I feel weary from the broken that is my life and that is this world. I am ready to see it all changed and redeemed. Lord, give me Your eyes. I do not want to be so consumed by the darkness that I forget the Light is there. I am just beyond tired. I am exhausted from fighting to find the joy and the beauty. And, maybe that is my answer for today. *Do not forsake me?* Of course. But, deep down, I think I know You have not and will not leave me. Maybe more than that, I need to simply rest in Your promises and in the reality that what You see is the whole, perfectly beautiful version of the things that are unseen to me. It does not change anything for today, but it does give me a glimmer of hope — strength for today and hope for tomorrow, Daily Bread. This is my prayer, God.

IF YOU WANT...

Look up the definition of forsaken and ask yourself this question: Do I feel forsaken by God? If the answer is yes, pray for the ability to see God in the story He is writing in your life today. If the answer is no, praise God for the grace to be able to know He is present, and pray for this to be a continual truth in your heart.

IF NOT...

Say these words aloud: Why, O, why, have You forsaken me, God?

Think about what that stirs in your heart and why.

For God, who said, 'Let light shine out of darkness,' has shone in our hearts to give the light of the knowledge of the glory of God in the face of Jesus Christ

2 Corinthians 4:6

"For God, who said, 'Let light shine out of darkness,' has shone in our hearts to give the light of the knowledge of the glory of God in the face of Jesus Christ"

2 Corinthians 4:6

I once had a roommate who had a picture of Jesus that hung on the wall beside her bed. I realize You know this, God, since You know all the things; but go with me here. We lived in the sorority house and one time, during a house tour, a recruit looked at the picture and proclaimed, "Bob Marley! I love him!" (Again, I know You remember this because You were there. But, for some reason it feels good to tell you again.) When my roommate told the new girl that the picture was Jesus, she was mortified! We all got a good laugh about it. But, I have thought about it several times since, particularly in this new chronic suffering. Your face in that photo was the same face I had seen in Sunday School as a small child. You had a slightly serious, partially smiling look about You. For certain, Your face looked kind. Lord, what did Your face really look like? I wish I could see You. It seems as if You were sitting right in front of me. Anything that seemed to distract me would take a backseat and we would just be together. I find it interesting that when I see drawings of You, Your face always has that same, somewhat emotionless, look to it. The more I get to know You, the more I think that could not be further from the truth. Jesus, in Your Word, You were always drawn to other people's pain. You hated the suffering, and You knew that You were the only way to relieve it. When I picture Your face, I want to see You as You really are. You are not a passive bystander, but a zealous Savior. Your power knows no limit. I would imagine that when You were hanging on the cross, Your face showed deep, excruciating physical pain. When You were weeping beside Lazarus' tomb (knowing very well both the temporal miracle that was going to occur, and the forever miracle of Your own death and resurrection on our behalf), I bet Your weeping was not soft and polite, but loud and uninhibited. Yes, You are kind and gentle. But, today when I picture Your face, I want to see it as the reflection of the Man of Sorrows. That is who You are, always willing to enter in with us. You are not repelled by our downtrodden countenance but deeply drawn to us in it. Lord, when I see Your face in the context my heart and mind, may I see You as You truly are. *The face of Jesus Christ* is the face of fully God and fully man. Help me to know You as You truly are.

IF YOU WANT...

Go to the Gospels and pick out a chapter (really, any chapter!) that includes Jesus interacting with other people. Picture His face in those moments. What does His face say about His heart toward us? Feel free to read as many stories as you are able.

IF NOT...

Pray these words: Lord, thank You that You are not a stoic, emotionless God; but instead, Immanuel, God with us.

Know and believe me and understand that I am He.

Isaiah 43:10

"You are my witnesses," declares the Lord, "and my servant whom I have chosen, that you may know and believe me and understand that I am He. Before me no god was formed, nor shall there be any after me"

Isaiah 43:10

Lord, sometimes it feels like I spend so much time thinking about who I am. It's not always in a spiritual sense; but, I think a lot about my roles, responsibilities and performance. I often base my day on how I meet certain expectations of myself or how quickly I can check things off of my to-do list. I also place so much weight on things I think those around me should do or even what they should be like. As I am reading through Isaiah 43, this phrase stands out more than most: *I am He*. When I see these words, I cannot help but think You are speaking to me. Who is He in the context of meaning here? Clearly, I know You are God. As I continue to read, I see many words that describe who You are: The One who created us. The One who formed us. The One who redeemed us. Really, I could stop there and find ample reason to praise You for being, "*I am He*." But, the chapter goes on: The One who calls me by name. The One who says, "You're mine." The One who is with me in the waters. The One who keeps me as I pass through the waters and walk through the fire. The Holy One. My Savior. The One who calls me precious and honored. The One who says, "I love you." The One who gave a ransom for me — Yourself. The One who is always with me. The One in control of all things. The One who formed and created us for His glory. The One who calls me His witness and wants all people to come to Himself. The One who chose me. The only Savior. The One whose work cannot be thwarted. My Redeemer. My King. The One whose way will absolutely happen. The One who quenches thirst in the desert. The One who formed us for His pleasure. The One who created us for His praise. The One who blots out all our sins out of His love for us.

Lord, when I read this, all I want to do is believe You are who You say You are. If this is You and You truly want to be with me forever, how could I not be left speechless, yet full of hope?! Even in the wilderness that is today, nothing makes sense but to come to You in praise. Would you help my heart to stay in this posture in all the moments that are to come? I do not know what this day holds, but You absolutely do. May I rest in the truth of who You are. Thank You for including me in Your glorious plan — a plan I do not yet understand, but that You promise works for good. I love You, Lord. May I trust in Your love for me more and more, and may I share this love with others.

IF YOU WANT...
Find Isaiah 43 and spend some time meditating on who God says He is.

IF NOT...
Choose one of God's attributes listed above that stands out to you and focus on that today.

But as it is, they desire a better country, that is, a heavenly one. Therefore God is not ashamed to be called their God, for He has prepared for them a city. —Hebrews 11:16

"But as it is, they desire a better country, that is, a heavenly one. Therefore God is not ashamed to be called their God, for He has prepared for them a city"

Hebrews 11:16

The grass is always greener on the other side.

I have heard this phrase since I was little, and it has always made sense to me. Lord, You know that even from a young age I have fought discontentment. It is always easier to look at someone else's life and think that if my own life looked that way, I might be happier. Sometimes these insecurities are even worse on the days that I look forward to the most. I get this eerie feeling after something I am excited about is over. Even if it has been an incredible experience, the same thing always happens: It ends. And, I am left with the reality that enjoyment always has an expiration date.

A better country.

Father, it seems that what You continue to say in Your Word is that yes, everything on this earth is perishing. Nothing here lasts. I think this is why, in love, You urge us to not fix our eyes or bank our satisfaction on the things that are here. Because of Your love for us, You know that the only satisfaction that we can truly find is satisfaction in You. I read it in Revelations — the times that You say that You are going to take all the sad things of this world and make them untrue, forever. Honestly, this sounds amazing, but hard to believe. My fear of being disappointed often causes me to not hold steadily onto Your promises. But, I want to hold onto You. I long to be in a place where discontent is nothing more than a dream from the past. And, if You did not put this longing in my heart, then where did it come from? I must believe that I was made for another Kingdom. It is the only thing that makes sense. Lord, would You help me to be brave in my trust of You? Give me the ability to hope. It is so hard to hope when it seems as if discouragement is around every corner on this side of Heaven. In some ways, it is the only thing we know here. But, I want to trust, and I want to believe that better things are coming because You promise them. Despite what I do not understand, would You help me to trust in the beliefs tucked deep down in my soul? This world just cannot be my home. Oh, may it be so. Help my unbelief. Cause my heart to see a glimpse of what is to come, and may that be manna for the day. Only You are able.

IF YOU WANT...
Read Revelations 21:1-6. Consider your current season of life. What about your current reality will not be in heaven? Write down the things *a better country* will not include for you that your earthly life does.

IF NOT...
Ask your heart this one question: Does my heart long for a better country?

You have kept count of my tossings, put my tears in Your bottle. Are they not in Your book?

Psalm 56:8

"You have kept count of my tossings, put my tears in Your bottle. Are they not in Your book?"

Psalm 56:8

I do not remember the last day that I did not cry. It feels like there is a constant lump in my throat, ready to overflow at any given moment. My face is puffy and swollen from the sadness. My skin is dry from the constant flow of hot tears that keep running down my face. I do not remember ever feeling an ache this deep.

Lord, where are You? No, really, I feel as if I continue to cry out to You, literally, and You answer me with Your silence. Is this how You treat those You say You love? Am I going to feel this way forever? There is no part of me that assumes You have forgotten me; yet, it feels even worse than that. It hurts my heart even more to think that You see all of this yet You are not intervening. Why, God? Why? I have never felt this alone. Pain and suffering are the most real things I know right now. It feels like it will never end. I know that is not true. Everything comes to an end, even the hurt. But, today I just do not see how this is all going to work out for good. It all feels so cruel.

As I sit here and think about the number of tears I have cried simply in this season of my life, I am in awe that You say You put them in Your bottle. Surely that must mean that they are each important to You. Even in the moments that I lack understanding of Your plan, You are doing something. Even when I try, I can't not believe that it is true. Even still, this is simply HARD. It is more excruciating than anything I can remember feeling before. I keep reminding myself that trials produce endurance and endurance produces hope. It is another promise of Yours that I just want to see the results of here and now. I hate this. I hate this overwhelming depression that feels like it is going to overtake me. Be near, God. When I think about Your book, I want to remember that even when I cannot see it, You are continuing to write the chapter and the Greater Story. Help me to remember that one day, I will have eyes that see all the beautiful things You were doing in this dreadful place. Today, it is just too much. Hold me now.

IF YOU WANT...
Read Psalm 56. Select a verse and draw a picture describing the verse as you envision it.

IF NOT...
Say these words: God, I am so tired of being so sad all the time. Please be my strength.

It is the fact that you are with me no matter what that spurs me to keep going.

Lord, I do not have the strength to open up my Bible today.

Everything feels foggy and I am exhausted — body, mind and soul. The only thing I am sure of is that somehow, You still have drawn me to Yourself in this moment. There are a few truths swirling around in my head: You are good. Your mercy endures. Your love is sure. You're faithful even when I am faithless. You are bringing beauty from ashes. I am not sure where these words are found; and I am positive You do not need me to reference Your own words for them to be real. Even so, I remember that somewhere in Romans 8 You promise that nothing can separate us. Does that nothing include weariness this big? I think it must. You even say that death cannot bring us apart. I have walked through a lot of darkness, but I have not yet crossed from this life through death. If You are on the other end of that, surely You are involved in everything in between. Lord, help me to trust You. I want to believe You are here, and even a mustard-seed desire feels hopeful. So often, I long for big feelings and clear passion. But, if I was always on the mountaintop, would there ever be any growth? Sometimes I hate that this is true, but it often seems that it is in the valleys that I learn most. It seems like it is in places like today that my flesh does not enjoy but my soul knows well You are carving out details of this story that are both necessary and eternally beautiful. God, why do I always feel the need to prove my relationship with You, both to myself and others? The hope of the Gospel is Your love for me, not the other way around. While I was a sinner — helpless and dead in my own mess — You died for me, not the other way around. It is the fact that You are with me *no matter what* that spurs me to keep going. Thank You for meeting me in this place. Thank You for never letting go. May I trust You more and more.

IF YOU WANT...

Make a list of the five most challenging aspects, things, relationships, struggles or losses in your life right now. Fill in the blank five times while writing this sentence:

(Put challenge here) cannot separate me from the love of God.

IF NOT...

Say this sentence aloud as many times as you want: God says nothing can separate me from His love for me.

For my thoughts are not your thoughts, neither are your ways my ways, declares the Lord. For as the heavens are higher than the earth, so are my ways higher than your ways and my thoughts than your thoughts —Isaiah 55:8-9

"For my thoughts are not your thoughts, neither are your ways my ways, declares the Lord. For as the heavens are higher than the earth, so are my ways higher than your ways and my thoughts than your thoughts"

Isaiah 55:8-9

Sometimes I forget that You do not just say that our ways and thoughts are a little bit different. No. You make it clear that Your mind and Your methods are not at all the same as mine. You are not just human with a little extra. You are God. You are the Creator who literally breathed and things came to be. These days, I feel like I am spending so much energy and time focusing on the why behind what You are doing. Everything human in me just does not get it. There is nothing about these trials that makes sense to me. Yet, You are my Father. A good parent does things that their children often do not like or understand. So, if Your ways are so far from mine that they are higher than I can even comprehend, I simply must trust that You are doing something. It is so far from easy — everything but easy, actually. Lord, I cannot do this on my own. I just cannot. It feels like one more breath, one more step forward in this journey is one too many. I need You. I need You to step in and, because You know the way that I am going, help me to stop trying to grasp *Your ways* and instead, choose to rest in You in the midst. You are always doing more than I could ever perceive. You are God alone. If I think about it, I would not want to worship a God whose knowledge and wisdom were fully able for me to obtain. Would You meet me here? I want to trust that despite what I see, You are able. The Enemy of my soul would love for me to believe that because it all seems bad, no good could be produced. Yet, deep down I know that is a lie. Your Spirit tells me otherwise. May I hear Your whisper in my soul louder than the noise around me. Lord, teach me to trust Your heart.

IF YOU WANT...

Read Isaiah 55. Write down and/or speak aloud all the invitations given to the reader.

IF NOT...

Is it comforting for you to know that God tells us His ways and His thoughts are much higher than our own? Why or why not?

But I call to God, and the Lord will save me. Evening and morning and at noon I utter my complaint and moan, and He hears my voice. He redeems my soul in safety from the battle that I wage, for many are arrayed against me

Psalm 55:16-17

"But I call to God, and the Lord will save me.
Evening and morning and at noon I utter my
complaint and moan, and He hears my voice.
He redeems my soul in safety from the battle that
I wage, for many are arrayed against me"

Psalm 55:16-17

I am feeling so empty inside. I woke up today unmotivated to get out of bed at all. The sheets feel warm and comfortable, the silence is inviting, and I am not looking forward to a single thing that this day holds. It all feels so mundane. And, I am tired, so very tired — the kind of exhaustion that seeps from the inside out and soaks into every area of my life like a sponge. What are we really doing here? Is this the abundant life? The disciples of old seemed to live a big adventure. As I read story after story about the lives of saints from the past, nothing about my daily life feels connected to theirs. How long, O Lord? Why does it always feel like something is missing?

But I call to God.

I read these words and feel a flicker of a flame within me. The Psalmist does not seem like someone who was always "feeling it." He goes back and forth on whether You are fully present in his life. And, every time, in ways that only You can, You seem to assure Him that You are there. I want to believe this, God. I want to trust that You hear my voice and that if You are not changing my circumstances or my perspective of them, it does not mean You are not doing something. Lord, help my unbelief. I am comforted that, in Psalm 55, it is said that complaints were uttered morning, noon and night — essentially, all day. So, if I begin this day with frustrations, continue it there, and then lay my head down with these same words, You will meet me. You want me to come to You as I am. While I wish I was waking up today with sunshine gleaming in my heart, it just is not so. Lord, I would love to experience joy today. Would You cause my heart to feel Your pleasure, regardless of my circumstances right now? *I moan.* I just do not have the words. I come to You and pour out my heart, trusting You will draw near. Oh, Lord, be near.

IF YOU WANT...
Meditate on Psalm 55. Which verse is most comforting to you today and why?

IF NOT...
What battle is your soul fighting today? Have a conversation with God about that battle.

Jesus answered him, "What I am doing you do not understand now, but afterward you will understand"

John 13:7

"Jesus answered him, 'What I am doing you do not understand now, but afterward you will understand'"

John 13:7

Lord, I do not understand what You are doing. I feel like I continue to come to You with these words, but I am not sure what I expect You to do about it. You have made it clear time and time again: I am not going to fathom Your ways. I know this in my head, yet my heart just does not want to accept it. It feels like if I knew what You were doing — or even if I could get a glimpse of the bigger picture — it would be easier to trust You. But, I guess faith would not be required then. Why is faith such a big thing, God? You know us. You know how weak we are in our own humanity. Oh, how I wish that I always felt the fullness of Your strength in me. I am realizing more and more that Your perspective through eternal lenses is the only view that will continue to spur hope deep within me. If I do not look at this world in congruence with the world to come, I am going to go into despair. I long to be able to confidently press on here in light of there. Why is that always so hard for me to do? The stamina of my faith doesn't ever last as long as I would like. Yet, You are God alone. I do know this. And, it is comforting to remember that Jesus made it clear that, one day, we will understand. When we see You face to face, we will know as we are fully known. What joy this brings! Oh, I long to believe this more deeply. I desire to see Your words, Lord — *but afterward* — and be propelled forward in hope. Lord, may it be so. Would You help my heart to have eyes that fixate on what is to come? This world is temporary. You are making all things new. Amid all that is heavy, cause my spirit to grab onto Your promises. Your love is sure. Would You meet me in this place?

IF YOU WANT...

What are you most excited about understanding in the Kingdom to come? What about the promise of future clarity brings you hope today?

IF NOT...

A prayer: Lord, there is so much I do not understand. Help me to trust that You know what You are doing, even when I do not. Amen.

For all the promises of God find their Yes in Him. That is why it is through Him that we utter our Amen to God for His glory

2 Corinthians 1:20

"For all the promises of God find their Yes in Him. That is why it is through Him that we utter our Amen to God for His glory"

2 Corinthians 1:20

Those words stand out to me like neon. God, there are so many beautiful promises in Your Word. I see message after message from You, telling us that we will prosper through You and You will bring us satisfaction forever. However, it seems the more life goes on, the more challenging it is to experience this in the everyday. And, although I see the "yes" strewn throughout this passage, the irony does not leave me. This season of life seems to carry no after no. I have prayed for so many things that You have, evidently in wisdom, answered with almost the opposite of what I have asked. Why is that? Am I so far removed from Your will for my life that Your interceding involves veering left when I have begged for right? I do not know the answer; but, I want to believe that You are working all for good. I desperately want to see You here.

I know, God.

"Why" does not seem to be the question I need to ask. Rather, "why" is usually not the deeper layer of what I need to know. Beyond that, I am not sure if I got Your answer that I would be able to comprehend it. More than anything, I long to believe Your ways are, in fact, higher. I desire to see Your love in a way that causes my heart to find rest in You instead of restlessness in the circumstance. This is what I truly need. So, if all Your promises are Yes in Christ, this means that I may not fully experience them face to face until I experience You face to face. It does not mean, however, that Your promises have failed me or that they are any less true. No. My vision is extremely limited, which is also why it makes sense that I am only able to say, "Amen" to what is in front of me when I do it through Christ. It is *through Him* I can see rightly. Jesus, You say that Your life is now mine. Help me to receive this more and more. You are already seated on the throne, and You say my true life is hidden with You! I do not have to see it to believe it is true. I do believe. God, help my unbelief.

IF YOU WANT...

Think back on your life thus far. What would your life look like if God had answered yes to everything you had asked of Him? Considering this, why does it bring you comfort to know all that He promises will always be fulfilled in Christ? How does this help You to trust Him more with your current desires?

IF NOT...

Say this phrase aloud: I can only say Amen to all God has done and is doing through Christ. When I cannot say Amen to what is in front of me, Christ can do that for me.

And after you have suffered a little while, the God of all grace, who has called you to His eternal glory in Christ, will Himself restore, confirm, strengthen, and establish you.

1 Peter 5:10

"And after you have suffered a little while,
the God of all grace, who has called you to
His eternal glory in Christ, will Himself restore,
confirm, strengthen, and establish you"

1 Peter 5:10

A little while.

That phrase is so relative. As a child, road trips that included the phrase, "not too much longer" tended to feel like ages. This suffering feels the same, God. I blush as I say this; yet, I have already thought it, so You know. You are aware that at the core of me, I find myself wondering about the length of Jesus' suffering versus the length of my own. I do not even know what I mean by that. Clearly, Lord, You deserved none of the pain You willingly took on. But, did I earn these trials? I know I am not entitled to anything, including the very breath in my lungs. But, I guess what I am really trying to articulate is that Your earthly hurt had an expiration date that sometimes feels like it was quicker than mine. I am embarrassed that these thoughts even exist in my mind — and more so, within my heart — yet I know they do. God, You created me. You were the One who loved me before the beginning of time. You gave me life and have offered me eternity. Surely I can trust You in this short-term affliction. The truth is, even if *a little while* lasts the entirety of my human life, it is still a blip compared to forever. Beyond that, the fact that You let me speak such authentic, borderline disrespect to You as I pour out the questions of my heart lets me know that Your love for me is beyond what I can comprehend. The God of the universe owes me nothing yet has given me everything. What undeserved grace. I want to be able to trust You in the here and now. True, Jesus, Your earthly life was 33 years. Still, You did not have to create me or, much less, come down and save me. While it is all still confusing and I do not feel like the answers all make sense, what I do know of Your love causes me to hold fast even in the midst of uncertainty. Lord, help me to trust You while I wait for the unseen. Help me to know that when it feels like chaos and it appears that evil is winning, I can still trust You. Thank You for Your constant love.

Come quickly, Lord.

IF YOU WANT...
Make a list of all the ways you have seen God restore, confirm, strengthen and establish you throughout your life. Keep that list in a place where you can continually look back and remember His faithfulness during times when it feels hard to see.

IF NOT...
A prayer: God, thank You that You say this pain I feel will not last forever. Amen.

The Rock, His work is perfect, for all His ways are justice. A God of faithfulness and without iniquity just and Upright is He — Deuteronomy 32:4

"The Rock, His work is perfect, for all His ways are justice. A God of faithfulness and without iniquity, just and upright is He"

Deuteronomy 32:4

I am struggling to believe that this is all Your perfect plan. I have tried to hold on to the truth for so many years. You promise me hope and a future. You tell me Your plans for me are good. Yet, how? Why did You make Your ways so far from ours? Why does it seem like there is nothing good that can come from this? If I am Your child, and if You long for me to be satisfied by You, then where is that satisfaction in the midst of this deep valley? My soul feels as dry as the desert. I am parched from the inside out. I do not see how anything holy could come from this, much less perfection.

Yet You.

You are God alone. You are holy. All the days were written before, yet one came to be and You have called this day good. I want to be able to praise You in this storm but, honestly, I am not sure how to do that. I do not have the strength to trust You in this place. Would You be my strength? You are the Rock I can both stand on and hide under. Be my firm foundation and my hiding place. Without You, I am nothing. Your word does not say my circumstance is perfect; or that the people around me or I have it all together. No. It is You. *His ways are perfect*. So, when I do not understand the script in front of me, may I trust the One controlling its scenes. Furthermore, You are the main character, not me! It is not about me, yet You promise me good. It is such undeserved grace. Help me to see You, yes, even here. On my own I cannot, but I know that You can do all things. God is God and I am not, and that is a good thing. May I believe this all the more.

IF YOU WANT...
Using a concordance or the internet, look up the word "perfect" in relation to the Bible. Meditate on all the places in Scripture that use this word; and, ask the Holy Spirit to reveal something to You during those meditations, as only He can.

IF NOT...
A prayer: God, I long for the day when I am able to see everything as you call it: perfect. Give me Your eyes to see even a glimpse, even here, even now. Amen.

Blessed is the man who trusts in the Lord

Jeremiah 17:7

"Blessed is the man who trusts in the Lord,
whose trust is the Lord"

Jeremiah 17:7

Here we are, back at that word again:

Blessed.

Why does it bring a look of disgust to my face each time I read it? I hate that a word commonly used in Christian vocabulary is repelling to me. But, Lord, You know. You are aware that something in my heart looks suspiciously — or maybe even enviously — at this word. It feels as if the world — even the church world, at times — looks at a blessing as something that has been far removed from my own life. It seems that being *blessed* has become synonymous with God answering prayers the way we want. This stings immensely because I have spent years asking for things You have denied. Lord, am I missing something? Do I need more faith to increase so-called blessings? I look around and feel ridiculous. There are many tangible things You have richly provided me with; yet, You have denied so many desires of my heart. God, I need to know what being *blessed* means in the context of You and Your Kingdom. Your word says *blessed* is the man whose trust is the Lord. This shifts things in my heart a little because I do long to make You my trust. You know this because You know me better than I know myself. And, while I fail at this daily, I also know that You see my heart and that You promise Jesus covers all. He is my righteousness. When I think of that in congruence with blessing, I realize that yes, I am already eternally *blessed*! Things are not as they seem. Just because I cannot see it does not mean it does not exist. You say that I am already *blessed* because I trust in You — no fine print involved. So, even when I feel as if I am missing out on the blessings, I can know that in the spiritual sense, not one of them is missing. I am *blessed* simply because You are everything, and this awareness of You changes everything. Lord, help me to have eyes to see what is unseen. Clearly, this is impossible without Your vision. I do not want to rely on what is in front of me. I long for my trust in You to deepen. Guide me deeper into Your truth, God. Only You are able.

IF YOU WANT...
Read Jeremiah 17:7-8. How have you defined *blessed* in the past? How does your definition compare to what these verses claim *blessed* is? How is it different?

IF NOT...
Ask God to redefine the meaning of *blessed* in your heart and in your mind.

How long, O Lord? Will You forget me forever? How long will You hide Your face from me? How long must I take counsel in my soul and have sorrow in my heart all the day? How long shall my enemy be exalted over me?

Psalm 13:1-2

"How long, O Lord? Will You forget me forever?
How long will You hide Your face from me?
How long must I take counsel in my soul
and have sorrow in my heart all the day?
How long shall my enemy be exalted over me?"

Psalm 13:1-2

This, all of this. I have never read words that feel truer. It is comforting that You included ressurance like this in Scripture. I am reminded that despite how it feels, I am not the only one who wonders how much longer their trials will go on. You are clear that endurance is needed in the Christian life. But, honestly, the amount of pain, waiting and lack of joy that I am experiencing just feels like too much. *How long* will I have to go on like this? I desperately want to sense You are in this. And, to be authentic, I just want relief sometimes. It seems like so many people, even those who consider themselves Christ followers, live with ease. They have their cake and eat it, too. Where does that leave me? I do not want to feel jealous of others' lots or suspicious of their hearts. That is not my place. Only You see hearts. God, help me to lay down my expectations of what is in front of me. Instead of spending my days wondering why, help me to look to You and know that You are with me, equipping me for whatever is here now and all that is to come. Right now, that all feels exhausting. The idea of even having one more moment in this deep darkness seems impossible. Again, Your Word says You can do the impossible. Help me to trust that You are strengthening me even when all I see is my own weakness. You promise to bring beauty from the ashes. I see so many ashes right now. Would You give me a glimpse of the beauty that is to come? You are God alone. May I trust You with my whole heart.

IF YOU WANT...
Read through Psalm 13. Insert the details of your current reality into the verses as you cry out to God with your own, "*how long.*"

IF NOT...
In your own words, tell the Lord why you feel forgotten.

I will lead...
I will guide...
I will turn the
darkness before
them into light...
these are the
things I do
Isaiah 42:16

"And I will lead the blind in a way that they do not know, in paths that they have not known I will guide them. I will turn the darkness before them into light, the rough places into level ground. These are the things I do, and I do not forsake them"

Isaiah 42:16

I find myself confused yet again. How am I supposed to trust that all things are in Your hands while also knowing there are real choices and tasks in front of me? If I believe You are sovereign — completely in control of everything — then where does that leave me? I do not think people are just pawns in Your hand. You displayed that in The Garden of Eden early on. We have decisions we seem to make and consequences for our choices. If there is a balance, where is it? It just seems odd that, at times, we are considered responsible for what feels like our own human limitations. I long to trust that You are working even in my own fumbling. I do not want to look at the road ahead, frozen in fear, believing it is all up to me. There is such mystery in this combination of You being the Ruler of all, allowing and prohibiting whatever You deem best, while also giving us a specific role to play. And really, what a privilege it is to be a part of the glorious script that is Your story. Help me to not mistake myself for the center of it all. Lord, I long to believe it is ultimately You accomplishing everything. You will lead us when we are in places unknown. You will guide us when we cannot see the way. You will carry us when the road is too tumultuous. You promise to never leave us. These are the things You will do. When I say I cannot, You respond, "Yes, I know. Yet *I will*." Amid all that appears to be so blurry in this life, may I cling to what I know to be true, to Who I know to be true. This broken world is not our home. You never once said that things would be easy. Yet, You gave us Yourself and that reality changes everything. May I trust in You today.

IF YOU WANT...

Read Isaiah 42. Write down who God says He is and what He says He will do within the context of this chapter.

IF NOT...

Pray this simple prayer: Lord, help me to believe everything is not up to me.

Why is my pain unceasing, my wound incurable, refusing to be healed? Will you be to me like a deceitful brook, like waters that fail? —Jeremiah 15:18

"Why is my pain unceasing, my wound incurable, refusing to be healed? Will you be to me like a deceitful brook, like waters that fail?"

Jeremiah 15:18

The longer this suffering drags on, the harder it is for me to trust You are on my side. I feel so alone. I feel so forsaken. It is becoming so hard for me to believe that You are going to bring good from what looks to me like a complete disaster. God, my soul knows You are good. I have seen Your faithfulness time and time again. But, God. Why add another layer of pain to my brokenness? It honestly feels like just too much. Feelings, feelings, feelings. You tell me that my heart is deceptive. If this is true, then why does it speak so loudly? I feel like if I do not get these things out, I am going to drown in them. Lord, help.

You know. You are more acquainted with me than I am with myself. I want to be able to simply rest in the reality that You are God and that You promise one day, this will all make sense. But, "one day" feels forever away right now. Lord, I need You more desperately than I know how to articulate. All other streams have failed. Nothing else is satisfying or comforting me. Would You give me a glimpse of Your sovereignty in this place? I do not want to doubt Your goodness merely based on how things seem to me. I want to believe You are present in all things. I do not want to think that You are *a deceitful brook*. No. I long to believe deep within who I am that You have always been and will always be The Fountain of Living Water. Help my unbelief. Draw me closer to You, God. I cannot do this on my own.

IF YOU WANT...

Do some research on different types of water, specifically looking at the definition of a brook. When you think about a deceitful brook, what comes to mind? What is the difference between a brook that fails and a brook that does not?

IF NOT...

Talk to God about where you feel like He is failing you.

The thief comes only to STEAL and KILL and DESTROY. I came that they may have LIFE and have it ABUNDANTLY

JOHN 10:10

"The thief comes only to steal and kill and destroy.
I came that they may have life and have it abundantly"

John 10:10

This ache in my soul is deeper than I know how to describe. How can a person feel so numb, yet have such incredible turmoil all at once? It feels like I have been in this place for longer than I can remember. How long, O Lord? This is the prayer of the Psalmist and it is mine, too. When I read John 10, I am so utterly confused. Your Word claims that the Enemy is what wants to steal, kill and destroy. You say that You offer me the most abundant *life*. Is that what this is? It feels like anything but fruitful and alive. I feel like I am dying a slow death from the inside out. Being dead honestly sounds appealing right now because it feels like the pain would be gone. Yet if it is *life* that You offer me — and if You still have me here — there must be something You are doing. I want to believe that Your plans for me are not simply good, but actually perfect. How am I supposed to trust this when all that is around and within me is so very bleak?

You came.

I read that part again and a glimmer of hope stirs in my heart. You came so that we could have the fullest *life* possible. And, while this life feels anything but full right now, the fact that You came must mean that You intentionally care. This does not change the intense suffering I am going through now; but, it does offer me a flicker of light for what You have in store. I am so grateful You do not ask me to hide my experiences of Your providence. I realize my perspective is limited, yet I am thankful You long for me to share everything with You. This is another aspect of You that makes Your love toward me evident. Help me to walk by faith, even when I cannot see where we are going. It is beautiful to think of You carrying me with confidence into what is to come. All the days were written by You before there was even a single moment. You promise to never leave my side. From the Garden to the grave and beyond, You are with me. Immanuel, God with us.

IF YOU WANT...
Read Matthew 5:2-12 and John 16:33. Does Jesus consider the abundant *life* a life of ease? How do you know? Why are we supposed to feel comforted by this?

IF NOT...
Think about what an abundant *life* means to you. Is your definition of an abundant life lasting or temporary?

Why do You hide Your face and count me as Your enemy?

Job 13:24

"Why do You hide Your face and count me as Your enemy?"

Job 13:24

I am so grateful I can say these kinds of things to You, God. Thank You for including the words of Job in Your book. I am thankful for the freedom to come before You honestly and tell You that, yes, it feels like You are treating me more like someone You hate than someone You love. I have tried my best to be faithful. I am human and sinful and messed up to the core; yet, You know this. You made me! And, based on what You tell me about Jesus, it is a lie to think that You are holding my transgressions over my head. But, if I am the created being and You are the Creator, why won't You help me? If this is Your version of help, why does it feel like I am being hit repeatedly? It seems like I get one small breath just to be thrown down again. This is all too much. I have said that before; and I have seen You sustain even there. Yet, this time, I honestly sense that I am completely drowning with no hope of coming up for air. And, honestly, a part of me does not want to take one more breath. Even if I just go to a place where I am unaware of anything, ignorance must feel better than the intensity and overwhelming darkness that seems like it just might overtake me at any given moment. Lord, be near. I am afraid of my current state. It feels completely out of my control. You say You are the Blessed Controller of all things. May I trust this even when everything around me gives way. Help me to reach out to others who will encourage me or — even better — would You cause someone to bring me even a glimpse of hope today? I want to trust You are working for my good. Why does it feel selfish to think that way? Those are Your words, not mine. May I believe they come from a place of unconditional love. Thank You for never giving up on me. When it seems like I am being treated like *Your enemy*, give me the ability to know that Your kindness is saturating my heart, whether I comprehend it in any given moment or not. Please be my strength.

IF YOU WANT...
Read Job 14. Which verses do you relate to most right now and why?

IF NOT...
Have you ever felt like God was treating you like His enemy? Spend some time talking to God about why or why not.

He has torn us, that He may heal us; He has struck us down, and He will bind us up.

Hosea 6:1

"Come, let us return to the Lord; for He has torn us, that He may heal us; He has struck us down, and He will bind us up. After two days He will revive us; on the third day He will raise us up, that we may live before Him. Let us know; let us press on to know the Lord; His going out is as sure as the dawn; He will come to us as the showers, as the spring rains that water the earth"

Hosea 6:1-3

Lately, I think a lot about Jacob. In Genesis 32, when he wrestles with God, there is this visceral quality about him. He seems to have no issue with seeing God — seeing You — as an opponent to be fought. I have read the story again and again, and still, I have so many questions. It is very obvious that You were not only fine with his wrestling, You actually blessed him for it. And, that blessing came in the form of a limp. When we emerge from deep waters, we often forget the lessons learned. Yet, when a tangible change occurs, the trials associated with it are not easy to dismiss. I would imagine that every time Jacob stood up, he remembered. It seems as if your version of a blessing simply involves this idea of constantly having eyes for that which is permanent — namely, You. The Bible is full of stories that include You allowing affliction. You make it very clear: affliction is a tool for Your glory. If this is true, then it seems that when we find ourselves in the middle of seasons of great pain, You long for us to be able to sense not the bruising, but the binding. When I think about this endless suffering we are experiencing, I am thankful You give me permission to say it is You that is in control of it all. *He has torn us.* While this may be true, may I not miss the second part. You only afflict when You are confident that greater healing will come from the affliction. This is a promise we can cling to in all things. I would much prefer to be able to experience the blessing without the hardship. Yet, You know. You are God alone and You determine what is needed. You are the Creator over all. When your methods seem harsh, may I remember that Your perspective is so much greater than my own. I want to trust You even when Your ways are confusing. Thank You for giving me permission to wrestle with You. I am so grateful You are not a god that asks us to be spoon-fed information and then simply accept it. No. You long for a relationship with us and want us to have the freedom to bring everything to You. What beauty is found, maybe especially in the most painful parts. Lord, help me to be like Jacob. What is interesting is he did not have the knowledge of Jesus that I do. Knowing what I know about Christ and what You have accomplished on my behalf, may I approach the throne with full confidence that You want me there. May I know that You do not break us for the sake of smashing us; but, for the sake of putting us back together with a wholeness we could never have experienced otherwise. Thank You for Your hold on me. Lord, be near. Keep these truths close to my heart today.

IF YOU WANT...

Go to Genesis 32 and read the story of Jacob wrestling with God. Which verse stands out to you the most right now and why? Do you have any limps, whether physically or holistically speaking, that you walk with? Have you learned to see it as a blessing? Why or why not? If not, what would it look like to view it as a gift instead of a curse?

IF NOT...

Spend some time wrestling with God today.

I cry out to God Most High, to God who fulfills His purpose for me

Psalm 57:2

"I cry out to God Most High, to God who fulfills His purpose for me"

Psalm 57:2

Oh, the depths of this pain. It hurts, God. Help. I am imagining myself laying helpless, bleeding out on the ground. I look up and see a supposed loved one. Oh, good, I think. Someone who can help. At first, I do not even make a noise. They will see me, I think. We make eye contact and they do nothing. So then, I start to speak. Again, nothing. Finally, I begin to shout and cry. I am in agony! I moan. But, still, no help, despite my cries.

This is how it feels right now, Father.

I assume it to be a grace that I believe You know my current condition. Where I feel most betrayed just so happens to be in that reality, however. Why are You not stepping in? Why are You not showing mercy and acting on my behalf? Your beloved needs You, God. How in the world am I supposed to feel like someone You delight in right now?

The cross. I know. Forgive me when I brush it all aside as if it is old news instead of the only news that matters. You did hang, literally bleeding out Your love for me. Why did Jesus not come down? Because He trusted that *His purpose* was greater than the sacrifice. His vision was completely different than mine. Was the process still excruciating? I would imagine, abundantly yes.

All of this is subjective to You. Whether I see it in any given moment does not change that reality. It seems all I can feel is anger right now. I am angry at having to trudge through these horrible moments day after day after day with no earthly relief in sight. I feel entitled to something better. In ways, that feels like a heavenly response if filtered through Jesus and His righteousness. But, right now, I just want things to be different. Lord, thank You for Your constant grace. I need You. Give me Your eyes today. This is so very hard.

IF YOU WANT...
Look up the definition of purpose. When you think of the purpose of God, what about the definition of the word "purpose" gives you a flicker of His presence today?

IF NOT...
A prayer: God, this hurts more than I know how to explain, and I am in desperate need of help.

It is enough

(1 Kings 19:4)

"But he himself went a day's journey into the wilderness and came and sat down under a broom tree. And he asked that he might die, saying, "It is enough; now O Lord, take away my life, for I am no better than my fathers"

1 Kings 19:4

Tears pool up in my eyes as I write this. Sometimes my heart hurts too much to cry. If the tears came out, I am not sure they would ever stop. I also do not even know the point of them. Why cry when nothing is changing? I put it on paper because I want to look back and know that You did something. God, I cannot do this anymore. The deep pain I feel inside scares me and feels like it threatens to overtake everything. I feel out of control in my own emotional state. If Your Spirit is stronger, I cannot go one more hour without seeing some sign of Your goodness in this. I do not remember ever feeling this weak and broken. Everything hurts from the inside out.

Oh, Lord, *it is enough*. I do not want to live anymore; but, live I must. The thought of taking my own life seems appealing at times; yet, I know that would not fix anything. Beyond that, the pain that would ensue in the aftermath for those that care (does anyone care?) sounds too harsh in an already jarring world.

The last thing I want to do is add pain onto pain.

Yet, escaping sometimes feels like the only way out of the chasm I find myself in. Elijah felt this. I read these words and they are a tiny drip of healing balm. I feel that statement — *it is enough* — with every ounce of my being. I wonder if, as Elijah was lying there, he had these same thoughts that I am having: How did I get here? Has it always felt this way? Lord, there is some place deep down within me (Your Spirit, maybe?) that seems to be speaking to me. A deep calls to deep, if you will. And, even though I am numb to even trying to believe it, somehow, I know You have not let go of me. It does not make me any less scared in this moment, though. Lord, be more near than ever before. Help.

IF YOU WANT...
Read 1 Kings 19. Put yourself in Elijah's shoes using all your senses. Imagine the scenario he found himself in. What does this story teach you about the character of God? How can you apply these truths to your own life today?

IF NOT...
Tell someone how heavy everything currently feels.

Oh Lord, why have you done evil to this people? Why did you ever send me? —Exodus 5:22-23

"Then Moses turned to the Lord and said, "O Lord, why have You done evil to this people? Why did you ever send me? For since I came to Pharaoh to speak in Your name, he has done evil to this people, and You have not delivered Your people at all"

Exodus 5:22-23

It is a question that comes up in my heart constantly, one that I am convinced You are never going to answer. So, really, the better question might be, *why* do I keep asking it?

I think it is because, in so many ways, it feels like my faith depends on it. I do not want to walk around thinking things and not sharing them with You. How can you have a good relationship with someone if you blindly accept confusing engagement without ever addressing it? It's funny. Throughout the Bible, You make it clear that You want for us to know You. The character of God is displayed and revealed over and over; yet, the *why* behind Your ways is so often hidden.

Why?

You would think that it would attest more to who You are if You simply disclosed a semblance of Your reasoning. Yet, as I write this, I realize that if that did happen, faith would not exist. If we understood everything You did, You would be no different than us, I guess. Beyond that, the beauty of who You are is often laid out in Your methods — the ones we do not initially grasp, yet tie together so very beautifully as they begin to unfold. I am not sure this season is going to do that. Honestly, I have massive doubts that You could bring anything good from what feels like a disaster of a time. Yet, You are God and I am not. I do not have to perceive this story from beginning to end — that is all You. In ways, when I think of it like that, it actually feels freeing to not apprehend the *why*. Maybe what I need most in this place is to find the strength within me to keep moving forward in the dark, trusting You are doing something. God, only You are able to help me to do that. Would You provide what I need in this moment? Lord, I need You. Oh, I need You. Every single hour, minute and millisecond, I need You. Be near.

IF YOU WANT...
Think back on your childhood and something that did not make sense to you at the time. Try to envision a particular story from your past that seemed impossible to understand then, but now makes sense to you. How does that help you to trust in the here and now?

IF NOT...
Continue asking God why.

Rejoice not over me, O my enemy; when I fall, I shall rise; when I sit in darkness, the Lord will be a light to me — Micah 7:8

"Rejoice not over me, O my enemy; when I fall,
I shall rise; when I sit in darkness, the Lord will
be a light to me"

Micah 7:8

My favorite thing about this verse is the word *when.*

Not if.

When.

Lord, I have fallen. So often, I worry whether I am going to give in to some temptation. I contemplate it in my mind, yet it never goes into action. Yet, this time?

I am in an absolute pit. I can see it for what it is, and also recognize that I am not sure I am ready to get out. There are things about falling that feel comfortable. If I am honest, the relief that I will feel if I simply cave in might be temporary, but it's something. And, right now, I feel desperate for any kind of consolation.

Yet, here is the thing. The shame I fight following sin makes the trial even worse. And even though I know You are still here, it is easier to believe the lie that You have somehow left me *when I fall.* God, I want to believe sin is not worth it. Beyond that, I really desire to see it for what it is — and to see You for who You say You are. My flesh is so very weak. Jesus, I remember You as You were being tempted by the Devil. You fought his deception with truth — the same truth You have given me. I know deep down that temporary fixes do not give me the peace I long for. Lord, I am sorry. Would you help me to see things rightly? Instead of just looking for the easy way out, would You cause me to have eternal vision — lenses that see things correctly? One day, I will know in full. I want to look back and see Your hand walking me through these trials, not my own hands reaching and grasping for fleeting pleasures.

Thank You for the grace You have offered me through Jesus — available even here, even now.

Help me to long for repentance, and in repentance, help me to rise.

Jesus, only You are able.

IF YOU WANT...
Do you have a "go-to" sin that you continue to lean on to try to relieve yourself from your pain? Bring that sin to the light and ask God to help you to see it for what it is.

IF NOT...
Admit that you have fallen and are in need of grace.

For this light momentary affliction is preparing for us an eternal weight of glory beyond all comparison

2 Corinthians 4:17

"For this light momentary affliction is preparing for us an eternal weight of glory beyond all comparison, as we look not to the things that are seen but to the things that are unseen. For the things that are seen are transient, but the things that are unseen are eternal"

2 Corinthians 4:17-18

There is a weight heavy on my chest, constantly pressing down. The only time I don't feel it is when I am asleep. As soon as I wake up, I sense it wrapping around my heart, like a suffocating blanket that won't let go. How could what I am walking through ever be seen as light? Did Jesus get back to heaven, look back on the cross and think, "No biggie. That was nothing"? It seems cruel to call someone's darkest pain irrelevant. Is that what these words mean, God?

Transient.

I think back on memories of my childhood. I remember ordering a pool float. You clearly know the one, God, if You know every word before it's on my tongue. I used all the prize money from some writing contest to get this island-themed inflatable. I just knew that it was going to be a game changer for my summer fun.

I could not have been more wrong.

It was pathetic. It was not sturdy, and it never even made it to the pool. I cried that day. Bawled, actually.

And, yes, regardless of how it all felt, I recognize it now as kind of ridiculous.

But, this? How can I see that float and this horrific trial as one in the same? I don't know. Yet, even as I write it, I am not sure that is what You are saying. After all, You wept when Lazarus died. You say that You care for all our cares. You call us to mourn with those who mourn. So maybe what You are saying here is not something along the lines of, "Stand up straighter and move on. This isn't a big deal." No. That has never been the way You have spoken to me. Maybe the reason You call it all light and momentary is because of what it is doing in the long run. After all, You clearly take suffering seriously enough to die for it. The truth is, my pain hurts You more than it does me. It may not always seem that way, but things are not always what they seem. You love me. If it matters to me, it matters to You. And, You promise me that this mess is *preparing* for me something that will hold weight for all eternity. Oh, Lord, give me Your eyes. I desperately need lenses that look beyond this season. Even as much, I long to be able to trust that this preparation is something to rejoice in — not because the affliction is any less hard, but because it is doing something greater than anything I could even imagine. I cannot yet see it, but I want to believe it. Lord, help my unbelief.

IF YOU WANT...
Read 2 Corinthians 4. How is it possible to not lose heart amid any circumstance?

IF NOT...
A prayer: Lord, help my unbelief.

Likewise the Spirit helps us in our weakness. For we do not know what to pray for as we ought, but the Spirit Himself intercedes for us with groanings too deep for words

Romans 8:26

"Likewise the Spirit helps us in our weakness.
For we do not know what to pray for as we ought,
but the Spirit Himself intercedes for us with
groanings too deep for words"

Romans 8:26

I am not sure anything has ever resonated with me more. *Too deep for words.* This is exactly where my heart is when I try to pray. Truly, I have nothing to say. I guess prayer is as much about listening to You, God, as it is speaking to you. But, the quiet makes me feel even more alone. Normally, I feel like thankfulness combined with requests flow out like water. Yet, right now, there seems to be a plug over my heart that will not budge, leaving me without anything to bring to the table. The verse above scares me a bit. It seems that the Spirit consistently molds my prayers to fit Your will. This used to relieve me; yet, with all this pain I have walked through, how is this supposed to comfort me? What You have allowed does not seem safe. And really, You have never once said that my circumstances will be safe anyway. You do promise to be my security, though; and I long to sense You being that in this great darkness. There is such a visceral sound to the word groanings. And, in this verse, it is not me that is wailing, it is You. This is deeply comforting to me right now because that suggests intense concern. God, You care greatly about whatever is going on in my heart and in my life. You have proven time and time again that You are going to step in on my behalf — Jesus, You being the most obvious. Spirit, You always intercede for me. Always. And when I am at my weakest and without words at all, You assure me of both Your presence and Your intentionality with all the details both now and forevermore. When I am speechless, You are still working. Your strength is shown best in my most fragile states. I have nothing to offer but myself, just as I am. May this offering bring You glory. Lord, be near.

IF YOU WANT...

Think about situations in your life when words were not needed. God does not audibly talk to us, yet He certainly speaks. Where do you most hear God communicating to you? Is it through His Word? Through creation? Through His providential design? As you go about your day, listen for God.

IF NOT...

Think about this: when you don't have the words, God is still speaking on your behalf.

He gives power to the faint, and to him who has no might he increases strength

Isaiah 40:29

"He gives power to the faint, and to him who has no might he increases strength"

Isaiah 40:29

Lord, sometimes — okay, oftentimes — I feel so needy. It seems as if all my prayers boil down to me asking You for something. I can feel guilty about this, but lately I am realizing that maybe this is just a part of the way our relationship works. You are delighted in our receiving of You! When I am at my darkest, unable to see any flicker of light, You long for me to come and rest. Many days, I have this subconscious background noise telling me I need to try harder. Yet, that is not Your voice. You simply ask me — command me, even — to receive Your love. Needy is not negative when what I need — who I need — is You. Trying to get the world to satisfy my ever-growing and always-changing whims is scary and shaky ground. But, bringing all my hurt, pain and mess to You, and letting You minister to me there, that is holy ground. Lord, I am so grateful that You are my Firm Foundation. When all around me gives way, *He gives* me the ability to continue on. That is who You are, Lord. God, the darkness has not lifted. My circumstances never seem to pan out the way I want them to, and I am so very weary of the brokenness that is the world. Yet, You. You are always here, never scolding me for my losing sight of the bigger picture. You are always there, ready to provide the glimmer of light — the Daily Bread needed to press on. Would You bind my wandering heart to Yourself, Lord? Would you cause my heart to just rest in You, instead of me trying so hard? Lord, I long to see Your face. I want to know fully, even as I am fully known. But, right now, this is what You have for me. And even in darkness, You are still God. You never let go of me. You are always holding me fast. I do not know much but I have seen this to be true. May I trust in Your presence today.

IF YOU WANT...
Read Isaiah 40:29-31. Think back on the ways that you have experienced power and strength showing up when you felt you could not go on. Ask God to meet you in your weariness today.

IF NOT...
Say this out loud: God is drawn to my needs, and He longs to meet them with Himself.

LAST THOUGHTS

I would love to think that you are now in a place where all the dark places feel illuminated. It would be nice if, here at the end of this book, you were experiencing the weight of your current story completely lifted. I somehow doubt that to be true for you because, frankly, it is not true for me either.

But a glimpse.

I am hopeful that you have begun to sense a flicker of the Flame you long to know.

I am expectant that even in your most bleak moments, you are fighting to believe God is still present.

I am prayerful that you know Him in a deeper way than you have before, not because of my own eloquent writing, but because of this authentic relationship that God has invited you into. This morning, I read a portion of The Message version of Romans 5:8 that says this:

"God put His love on the line for us by offering His Son in sacrificial death while we were of no use whatever to Him."

This might be the best news we will ever read.

If you are feeling "of no use whatever to Him," rest easy.

His love for you supersedes any state you may find yourself in — past, present, future.

Nothing can separate You from the Light that overcomes the darkness.

Not even you.

I would love to leave you with a prayer on behalf of all of us who find ourselves wading in the murkiest waters — both the circumstantial ones and the ones of our hearts and minds.

May we know He is with us always and forevermore, even in darkness.

A PRAYER

God, we are so ready for the invisible to be made visible. The darkness we continue to come up against feels chronic and immense. We are wearier than words can express. Yet, You call Yourself Immanuel: God with us. As we attempt to put one foot in front of the other, would You usher us into the rest that is Your presence? Would You give us eyes to see the Greater Story that is being written, even here, even now? Thank You that because of Jesus, we can enter Your throne room with freedom and confidence. Thank You that Your Word is full of people and situations that remind us You simply want us to come as we are. You long for us to know that we are loved. Help us to not only acknowledge this, but to be changed by it. May we overflow with the power that comes from knowing the Light is always greater. Teach us to find beauty in being held by the Steady Love that is You. Only You are able, God. Until our faith has eyes, give us the strength to trust You.

Amen.

your
turn

WRITE A VERSE HERE:

_____

TALK WITH GOD

_____

_____

_____

_____

_____

_____

_____

_____

_____

_____

_____

_____

WRITE A VERSE HERE:

_____

TALK WITH GOD

_____

_____

_____

_____

_____

_____

_____

_____

_____

_____

_____

_____

_____

_____

WRITE A VERSE HERE:

_____

TALK WITH GOD

_____

_____

_____

_____

_____

_____

_____

_____

_____

_____

_____

_____

_____

_____

ABOUT THE AUTHOR

Morgan Cheek is passionate about seeing God in all things and inviting others to do the same. She is a wife to Hugh, a mother to two in heaven (Bailey Grace and Ally) and one on earth (James). She lives in Birmingham, Alabama; and when she is not reading or writing she is probably doing something active- whether outdoors or in the Orange Theory studio. Morgan is also the author of, "On Milk and Honey: How God's Goodness Shows Up in Unexpected Places" and, "Are We There Yet? One Sojourner's Journey Through Dross Consumed and Gold Refined". She co-hosts the podcast, Grief Sown. You can find the musings (and hopefully) encouragements of her own heart and life on Instagram (@seedsandleaven).